M000168990

250 total dots

⚠ = Begin a new line section.

⊙ = Pick up your pen/pencil and look for the next sequential
number with the small triangle symbol next to it.

269 total dots

⚠ = Begin a new line section.

⊙ = Pick up your pen/pencil and look for the next sequential
number with the small triangle symbol next to it.

446 total dots

▲ = Begin a new line section.

⊙ = Pick up your pen/pencil and look for the next sequential
number with the small triangle symbol next to it.

413 total dots

⚠ = Begin a new line section.

⊙ = Pick up your pen/pencil and look for the next sequential
number with the small triangle symbol next to it.

323 total dots

⚠ = Begin a new line section.

◉ = Pick up your pen/pencil and look for the next sequential
number with the small triangle symbol next to it.

394 total dots

△ = Begin a new line section.

⊙ = Pick up your pen/pencil and look for the next sequential
number with the small triangle symbol next to it.

407 total dots

⚠ = Begin a new line section.

⦿ = Pick up your pen/pencil and look for the next sequential
number with the small triangle symbol next to it.

322 total dots

△ = Begin a new line section.

◉ = Pick up your pen/pencil and look for the next sequential
number with the small triangle symbol next to it.

451 total dots

⚠ = Begin a new line section.

⊙ = Pick up your pen/pencil and look for the next sequential
number with the small triangle symbol next to it.

444 total dots

△ = Begin a new line section.

⊙ = Pick up your pen/pencil and look for the next sequential
number with the small triangle symbol next to it.

468 total dots

⚠ = Begin a new line section.

⊙ = Pick up your pen/pencil and look for the next sequential
     number with the small triangle symbol next to it.

474 total dots

⚠ = Begin a new line section.

⊙ = Pick up your pen/pencil and look for the next sequential
number with the small triangle symbol next to it.

342 total dots

⚠ = Begin a new line section.

⊙ = Pick up your pen/pencil and look for the next sequential
number with the small triangle symbol next to it.

334 total dots

⚠ = Begin a new line section.

⊙ = Pick up your pen/pencil and look for the next sequential
    number with the small triangle symbol next to it.

493 total dots

⚠ = Begin a new line section.

⊙ = Pick up your pen/pencil and look for the next sequential
number with the small triangle symbol next to it.

470 total dots

⚠ = Begin a new line section.

⊙ = Pick up your pen/pencil and look for the next sequential
number with the small triangle symbol next to it.

524 total dots

⚠ = Begin a new line section.

⊙ = Pick up your pen/pencil and look for the next sequential
number with the small triangle symbol next to it.

469 total dots

⚠ = Begin a new line section.

⊙ = Pick up your pen/pencil and look for the next sequential number with the small triangle symbol next to it.

⚠ = Begin a new line section.

⊙ = Pick up your pen/pencil and look for the next sequential
number with the small triangle symbol next to it.

293 total dots

▲ = Begin a new line section.

⊙ = Pick up your pen/pencil and look for the next sequential
number with the small triangle symbol next to it.

△ = Begin a new line section.

⊙ = Pick up your pen/pencil and look for the next sequential
number with the small triangle symbol next to it.

401 total dots

⚠ = Begin a new line section.

⊙ = Pick up your pen/pencil and look for the next sequential
number with the small triangle symbol next to it.

420 total dots

⚠ = Begin a new line section.

⊙ = Pick up your pen/pencil and look for the next sequential
    number with the small triangle symbol next to it.

364 total dots

⚠ = Begin a new line section.

⊙ = Pick up your pen/pencil and look for the next sequential
number with the small triangle symbol next to it.

504 total dots

⚠ = Begin a new line section.

⊙ = Pick up your pen/pencil and look for the next sequential
    number with the small triangle symbol next to it.

487 total dots

⚠ = Begin a new line section.

◉ = Pick up your pen/pencil and look for the next sequential
number with the small triangle symbol next to it.

496 total dots

△ = Begin a new line section.

⊙ = Pick up your pen/pencil and look for the next sequential
number with the small triangle symbol next to it.

356 total dots

⚠ = Begin a new line section.

⊙ = Pick up your pen/pencil and look for the next sequential
     number with the small triangle symbol next to it.

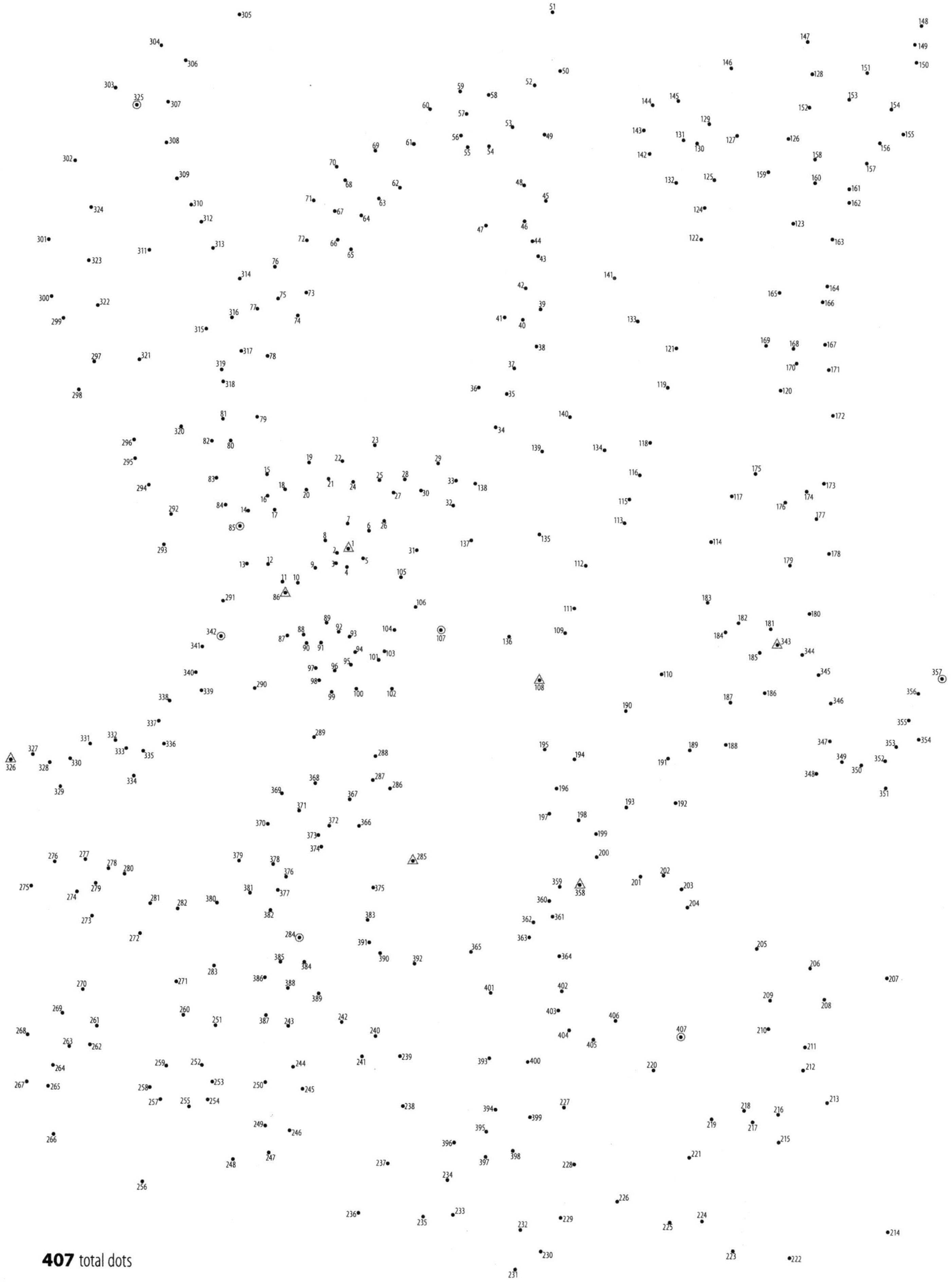

407 total dots

⚠ = Begin a new line section.

⊙ = Pick up your pen/pencil and look for the next sequential
number with the small triangle symbol next to it.

SOLUTIONS

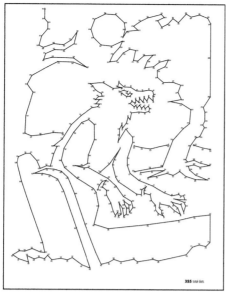

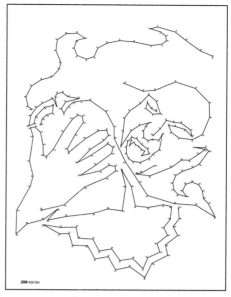

Plate 1 — Werewolf

Plate 2 — Vampire

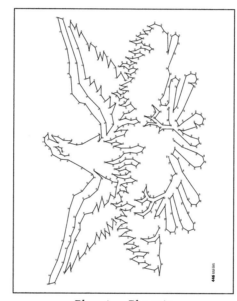

Plate 3 — Unicorn

Plate 4 — Phoenix

Plate 5 — Pegasus

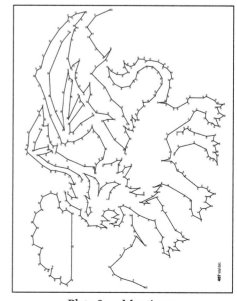

Plate 6 — Mermaid

Plate 7 — Minotaur

Plate 8 — Manticore

Plate 9 — Loch Ness Monster

Plate 10 — Griffin

Plate 11 — Gorgon

Plate 12 — Dragon

Plate 13 — Cyclops

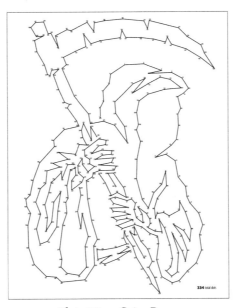

Plate 14 — Centaur

Plate 15 — Grim Reaper

Plate 16 — Sasquatch

Plate 17 — Basilisk

Plate 18 — Zombie

Plate 19 — Wendigo

Plate 20 — Typhon

Plate 21 — Sphinx

Plate 22 — Seagoat

Plate 23 — Orthrus

Plate 24 — Ogre

Plate 25 — Mothman

Plate 26 — Wizard

Plate 27 — Genie

Plate 28 — Mummy

Plate 29 — Arachne

Plate 30 — Harpy